Get Your Underachiever into College

*Parent Tested Strategies for
Struggling High School Students*

B. A. King

Get Your Underachiever Into College

Parent Tested Strategies for Struggling High School Students

Copyright 2019

Cypress Point Press

First Edition

Disclaimer

This book is not intended as a substitute for the medical advice of physicians or therapists. The reader should regularly consult a physician in matters relating to his/her child's health and particularly with respect to any symptoms that may require diagnosis or medical attention. Nor is this book a substitute for an educational consultant who knows your child's situation personally and, thereby, can offer specific advice and guidance.

No part of this book may be copied or transmitted by any means without the author's permission.

ISBN: 978-1-7335369-3-6

Dedication

To my children through whom I gained the knowledge

I am now passing onto other parents.

Author's Note

It is my sincere hope that the information in this book helps you guide your child to their best self. I often found while going through my own struggles, that it was a word from a parent who had experienced my difficulties who gave me the best advice. Unfortunately, I would pick up the advice piece meal which meant the next step was left in question. With this book, I tried to give you the entire plate full at once, at least as I know it. My husband and I always wanted to keep our kids supported until the light bulb went on. And when it went on, we wanted them to be in a place where they could move ahead successfully. So, put your faith in the process like we did. The process will prove itself.

Contents

Author's Note iv

Preface 1

How to Use This Book 6

What Is an Underachiever 7

Why Are Some Students Underachievers 8

    Learning Disability 9

    ADHD 10

    Executive Functioning Skills 11

    Maturity 11

    Confidence 12

    Motivation 13

    Stress 14

    Anxiety 15

    Mental Health Issues 15

    Substance Abuse 16

Getting to the Root of the Problem 17

High School—Off to a Good Start 19

    Testing 21

    Which High School 22

    High School Course Placement 24

    Educational Consultant... 25

    Tutor 26

    Academic Assistance 27

    504 Plan 29

    Parental Support 30

    Activities 31

Tactics to Consider 34

    Self-Discipline 34

    Study Space 35

    Use Incentives/Rewards.. 36

Not Ready for Prime Time—
Students on the Decline... 37

    Home School 38

    Night School... 38

    Special State High Schools 39

    Out-of-District Schools 40

    Private Schools 41

Students on the Decline—
Post-High School Options 42

    Community College... 42

    Local College or University 44

    The Thirteenth Year 45

    Small Steps for Gaining Momentum 48

Students on the Rise 49

    Pygmalion Effect/What Helped
    Turn Dave Around 49

    Power of Maturity 50

    Getting Support Important 52

    Increase Schedule Strength
    through Honors and Aps 53

Handling the College Application 55

    College Search Resources 55

    Educational Consultant for College......................... 58

    Going for Strengths.. 59

    Rolling/Priority Applications 60

    Sports Recruitment... 62

    Semester Grade Reporting 63

    Admission Statistics... 65

- Small vs. Large College 66
- How Colleges Evaluate Applicants 67

Resources for Choosing a College 69
- Naviance 69
- Princeton Review 70
- US News Colleges 70
- Colleges That Change Lives Book 71

College—Setting Stage for Success 72
- Grad School Tutors 72
- eTutoring 73
- Living Learning Communities 74
- Team 75
- Attendance Requirements 77
- Good Fit 78
- Outside Region 79
- Setting: City vs. Country 79
- Large vs. Small Engineering Schools 80
- 3/2 Engineering 82
- Explore College Websites 83
- Pre-college Programs—Turtle Camp 85

It's Time to Go to Work 87

    Role of Internships 87

    Getting the Job 88

Conclusion 90

Author Bio 93

GET YOUR UNDERACHIEVER INTO COLLEGE

Preface

You probably picked up this book up because you have a child who is an underachiever and you fear that he or she will never be successful. And he/she won't be if you do not take steps to intervene and plan his road map. This is no time to leave things to chance. There is too much at stake—your child's future. I know—I've I have been there.

This is not your average college prep book. Instead, this is about what I have learned firsthand to help my underachiever sons become successful in college and the work world beyond. I have also been actively involved with young people—mostly boys—for many years and have learned what works and what doesn't. In addition, I spent untold hours doing research to help my sons. Many times, just one tip was buried in a mound of reading—it took forever to find it. But I was persistent, so I did. Had I not had the time, ability, or determination to find the information I desperately needed, my sons might not be where they are today—one is a civil engineer, the other a mechanical engineer. I want to save you from all that trouble. A lot of time was lost searching for answers rather solving the problem.

This book will help you:

Identify the problem and your child's weaknesses

Discover your child's strengths

Plan strategies with the goal in mind

Recover from setbacks

Achieve college success for your child

How do I know the strategies in this book work? Because I am the mother of two underachievers. I actually have three children—two boys and a girl in the middle. One year early in their school careers, I had all three teachers' conferences in the same week. I heard about difficulties only with the boys—ages three and six at the time. But my four-year-old daughter, according to the teacher, was the star of her preschool class. It was foretelling. From that point, little changed in their grade-school careers. My daughter eventually went on to graduate from an Ivy League college.

My oldest son, Mike, was 2 1/2 years old when he was diagnosed with a language problem. The speech therapist told me he was not just behind but was also having difficulty acquiring speech. He did not understand the encoding of the language. That began our odyssey into the world of learning disabilities. Mike began speech therapy immediately. Then at age 6, his first-grade teacher, a reading specialist, discovered that his difficulty learning to read was due to his difficulty with the encoding of the language. That pronouncement prompted an immediate evaluation, which resulted in a language learning disability diagnosis. Much to our surprise, Mike did pretty well through grade school. But in freshman year of high school, he began to tank. We took him for another evaluation. This time, he was diagnosed with ADHD and started on medication to help him learn. It wasn't the magic bullet. Unfortunately, due to his immaturity, he never performed up to his ability in high school. After graduation, he went on to a postgraduate year before entering college where he majored in civil engineering. The first year of college he gave a middling performance at best. But the first semester of sophomore year, he made the Dean's List and was on his way. Today he is employed by a large construction firm in the Washington, DC area where he is proving himself to be an achiever. It wasn't easy to get him to this point. We tried many strategies—some worked, some didn't. But in the experimenting, we finally got the formula right.

My younger son, Dave, also had his struggles in school but he presented a bit differently. Dave started preschool a couple of months before his third birthday. His speech was almost unintelligible even to me. By the time he was four, he didn't want to go to school. I have wondered if his speech had set him up for a negative experience. Even if teachers tried to understand him, kids probably didn't spend the time. I often found him playing off in the corner by himself. Even so, I expected Dave to be an academic. He was intellectually curious and as he grew, he became a voracious reader and watcher of educational programs—mostly science oriented. By sixth grade, he started to crash. At that point, he was diagnosed with ADD and put on medication. While the meds helped him focus in the classroom, they did little to get homework done. His first semester of high school was dismal—that is when more intervention was needed. He was put into an academic support class and we double-teamed him with a tutor at home. The turnaround was put in motion.

Dave became a student on the rise. He started earning better grades and strengthening his schedule with honors classes. He made CAPT (Connecticut Academic Performance Test) scholar in sophomore year. Dave was accepted into his first-choice college and invited into a themed-based honors program. He graduated with a degree in mechanical engineering. Again, all of our intervention and strategies paid off.

It is not just my own sons with whom I have been involved. During my 20 years as a Boy Scout leader, I have known many boys for numerous years of their lives through weekly meetings, campouts, and lengthy summer adventures. Parents have shared their concerns and successes, and I have personally witnessed many boys transform during the course of their development, due to various strategies and interventions included in this book.

Remember, there is always hope for the future. Never think it is too late. The brain is still developing until nearly age 30. Children are resilient, too. We can make mistakes when trying to rear them, but children can come back from those poor choices. You, as a parent, can make a different, better choice next time. And your child will respond if it is the right one.

It is best if you start identifying problems early and searching for solutions. However, oftentimes, the problem reoccurs in a new form year after year. It is like being lost in a maze. You find one way out only to take a turn that leaves you lost again. But you have to keep trying because a child may be internalizing the solutions even if he or she is not yet performing outwardly.

The most important thing to keep in mind is to remain available to your child. You do this by maintaining a good relationship. And that does not mean you can never disagree, restrict, or punish. It means you remain engaged. By maintaining active involvement with our children, they have always come to us with their problems, whether it is a failing grade or something worse. Parents are much better problem solvers than friends.

How to Use This Book

I tried to make this book as user-friendly as possible. When you are desperately seeking a solution to your child's problem, you want to cut to the chase. And I hope the format I have created will allow you to do that. Consequently, I have repeated information in various sections of the book since you may skip around between chapters. The Table of Contents should help you navigate quickly. You can easily locate information you need without having search through the entire book. However, I hope you will, as it is important since you will get a stronger overall scenario of your child's problems and be better able to strategize his or her future. In fact, I recommend you start your plan with the end objective in mind. If it is your goal for your child to earn a college degree, then everything you do should support this. For instance, when considering a gap year for my oldest son, we knew he needed to be in school so he would continue onto college. Another choice might have taken him in a different direction. We wanted our child to complete his education before he began exploring the world. You know your child best, so you may want to make a different choice. Strategies that bear the end in mind will be the most successful in achieving your goal.

What Is an Underachiever

An underachiever is simply what he appears to be—someone who has greater potential than his performance indicates. In the case of school, potential may be measured by an IQ test. Or maybe there has been a brief glimmer of promise such as an outstanding essay or the solving of a complex mathematical problem. But the success is not maintained. Thus, the promise is never realized.

Oftentimes, as underachievers enter the teenage years, telltale signs emerge—he misses class more regularly, he does not turn in homework on time, and he has lost interest in learning. When report card time arrives, the underachievement is there in graphic form. It is undeniable. But why is this happening? Is it just a phase or something more? Let's explore and try to find out.

Why Are Some Students Underachievers

My older son, Mike, was an underachiever, a student whose ability and performance were separated by a wide gap. As is often the case, signs showed themselves early. He had speech/language problems beginning at two years of age. The speech therapist told me he was not only behind in language development, but he was also having trouble acquiring language because he didn't understand the encoding. He worked with speech therapists for several years. Then in first grade, his teacher—a reading specialist—stated that Mike was having difficulty learning to read because he did not understand the encoding of the language; there it was again. Mike did not understand the encoding of the language. But I did not understand what that meant. Upon receiving this news, I took him to reputable psychologist to be tested. The psychologist who evaluated him told me that she had never seen such a large gap between ability and performance. Consequently, Mike was diagnosed with a language learning disability that involved processing skills. I was concerned that Mike would have a lot of difficulty learning in school. But, much to my surprise, the early grade school years were fairly easy for him. As is often the case with bright students, he was able to compensate—getting by on his intelligence and memory skills. While a project may have presented some difficulty due to planning, organization, and time management, he would always be saved by the test. Even in middle school, he did fairly well, and received recommendations for honors math, honors science, and Spanish 3 in high school. But everything started falling apart in ninth grade. More testing revealed he also had Attention Deficit Hyperactivity Disorder (ADHD). Students with ADHD have brains that lag behind in development. Their executive functioning skills which involve organization, planning, and execution may be years behind their peers.

Let's look at the issues that impact achievement.

Learning Disability

Certainly, there are many different types of learning disabilities that can affect school performance and the more the demands, the harder it is for the student to perform. Basically, there are three categories of learning disabilities: development speech and language disorders, academic skills disorders, and other types involving such skills as coordination, penmanship, spelling, and memory. But when the disability affects the core of learning itself—such as a language disability—learning becomes especially difficult. If you think about it, most learning from grade school through high school involves language skills. First, you need to learn to read and write. And then, you apply those skills to various subjects—even math. As school progresses, there are more and more demands on those skills as they are developed in the peer group. In high school, Mike had particular difficulty with English. It started with the book selections—most of which held little interest for him. Of course, he resisted reading the books. I even tried getting books on tape when they were available. That helped somewhat but if the content was "boring," he was not interested in listening. Class discussion of the books also presented problems for him. Mike's processing speed was not fast enough to both listen and participate in the discussion. It is no wonder he learned to dislike English and did not do very well.

As I mentioned, some learning disorders involve communication, reading, writing, arithmetic, and motor skills. Many people have heard of dyslexia, which impacts reading. However, some people even go on to graduate law school using alternative learning strategies such as books on tape. A more insidious learning disability that I had never even heard of until my sons were in school is Attention Deficit Hyperactivity Disorder (ADHD). Attention Deficit Disorder (ADD), without hyperactivity, is also common and even more difficult to discern. Since ADHD is one of the learning issues that most impacted my sons, I am going to discuss it more in depth. However, ADD is now almost a household word, which many professionals have weighed in on over the years.

ADHD

This is a neurodevelopmental psychiatric disorder that impacts the ability to focus and may involve hyperactivity or impulsiveness. It is managed through lifestyle changes, counseling, and medication. It can accompany academic skills disorders and may be comorbid with other psychiatric problems such as depression. After freshman year in high school, Mike was diagnosed with ADHD and put on medication. The pill was not a magic bullet. It may have improved his concentration in class, but it did not result in getting homework done. He still did not have the study skills to complete his homework. And it is not because he wasn't taught study skills. Our school system really emphasizes this. In addition, we had sent Mike to a special study skills workshop right before high school. None of it seemed to help. Then we learned from our educational consultant that he had nearly nonexistent executive functioning skills.

Executive Functioning Skills

These skills impact planning, organization, and the ability to start and complete an assignment. Children with ADD often lag three years behind their peers in developing these skills. When you think about it, executive functioning skills are really key to success in school. You need these skills to manage nightly homework and plan ahead for projects.

The good news is that as students mature, the skills mature along with them. Both of my sons now have superb executive functioning skills. In fact, at times they are hyper-organized—not a bad thing considering the alternative.

Maturity

Many underachievers are immature both physically and mentally. In our school system, many students go through puberty before high school. Boys who develop later can lag in achievement. Maturity also affects brain development. Students with ADD, for instance, can have underdeveloped brains as late as their mid-twenties. When Mike was a senior engineering student in college, he told me that as he moved further along in engineering, it grew easier for him while most students felt it became harder. One explanation for this is that while his peers had more fully developed brains when they entered college, his brain was still developing and as it matured, the class work was easier. Not only that, his executive functioning skills had also matured.

Confidence

Some students become underachievers because they lose confidence in themselves. This can happen early in life. My younger son, Dave, stopped wanting to go to school when he was four. By the time he was in his repeat year of kindergarten, he was literally falling apart. Why was that happening? When I look back on it, I think he started preschool at too young an age. He wasn't even three. Besides, he had speech-language problems, which impacted his ability to participate and interact well with the other kids. I believe his early school experiences set the course for most of his grade school years. Dave continued to avoid school as much as possible until high school where attendance was required to pass courses.

My older son, Mike, lost confidence later—in high school. Not a good time to have this happen. Even though Mike had more learning issues than Dave, he always wanted to go to school to see the kids—he had a need to socialize. I think he always saw himself as rather smart. In eighth grade, he had to take a test to get recommended for science honors and he passed. He was so proud of himself. He was also recommended for math honors. Unfortunately, he started slipping in the last half of eighth grade. So, I decided it would be best to put him in regular classes where he would have a chance to excel, rather than honors where he might fail. Looking back, this may not have been the best course for Mike. I sometimes think he started to see himself as a less capable student because he was no longer grouped with the high achievers. Then, when he was placed in an academic assistance class sophomore year, I think he looked around the room and realized the group of underachievers and struggling students were his peers. No matter how hard we tried, we were not able to raise his self-image. It was not until his postgraduate year that he regained confidence in himself as a learner. As he progressed in college, he continued to gain confidence as he mastered tough engineering concepts and was rewarded with top grades. There is nothing like confidence to fuel success. Without confidence, it is difficult to do anything well. Avoidance behavior, which both of my sons exhibited, is a real tip-off of low confidence and self-esteem.

Motivation

Motivation comes with confidence. It is difficult for anyone, especially a child, to do anything they do not feel good about. The best way to develop motivation is through success or by appealing to an interest. People are more likely to read if they are reading something in which they are interested. Students are more likely to perform for a teacher who has made them feel successful. Dave received a comment on a paper from his sophomore English teacher, which was a turning point in high school. She wrote, "I like how you think." That one comment raised Dave's self-esteem and he began seeing himself as someone with good ideas—ones that were worth sharing in class and on paper. Teachers can have a powerful influence on a student's life. A few words from them can build confidence and motivation or it can send them into a downward spiral that could take a long time to reverse. If you look at high achieving students, you can't help but notice their motivation. They have confidence that years of positive feedback, many As, and community recognition have provided. Not so with underachievers. However, with the proper strategies, these students can be turned around and motivated to learn. Sometimes, they only need one person who believes in them.

Stress

We all know in today's world there is a lot of pressure on kids to succeed. They often react differently to stress. My son, Mike, became extremely social—he always had to be surrounded by his friends. Unfortunately, underachievers usually seek out those like themselves, so they are able to feel better and that doesn't help raise the bar or motivate them to change. Some students turn to activities that can have detrimental effects, such as alcohol and drugs. We must keep in mind that even negative behaviors are a symptom but not necessarily a cause. Today, many underachievers turn to video games. Some professionals consider video games one of the causes of underachievement. Is it a cause or only a symptom? Certainly, if a child spent that time on school activities, he would improve. My experience with my boys and the boys I have watched seems to be that video games are a way to relax and even gain some self-esteem if your skill allows. All of these behaviors are common to normal teenagers. It is just that underachievers may be extreme, so it is best to be vigilant.

Anxiety

Certainly, anxiety can be a result of too much stress. Often, too, it is comorbid, which means it exists simultaneously with other conditions including ADD. In fact, ADD medications often contain drugs that lessen anxiety. It would be natural for an underachiever to experience anxiety in a classroom where he is unprepared or feels intellectually challenged. Now that Dave is older, he is finally expressing he has social anxiety. When you are not comfortable in your own skin, it can be difficult to participate in class and do other things that would raise performance. Psychologists are trained to deal with this problem utilizing various techniques. Medication can also help initially until new behavior is learned. Some personality types are more prone to anxiety than others. And some can only take stress up to a certain point. Talking to your child and seeking professional help can determine their anxiety triggers. Then you can begin a plan to minimize them.

Mental Health Issues

Mental health issues must be identified and dealt with by your medical team. Certainly, mental health issues can impact students' ability to learn. Depression is probably the number one culprit, and it impacts confidence and motivation. School professionals even talk about "situational depression." A child can be depressed only in a school setting. Perhaps, but I don't really know. However, children can certainly shut down and appear to be depressed. If you think depression or another mental health issue may be your child's problem, I urge you to get help. The strategies in this book will not be enough to remedy your child's situation. With the right type of therapy and guidance, your child will learn how to become an achiever.

Substance Abuse

Substance abuse problems parallel underachieving. What came first, the chicken or the egg? Often times, underachievers turn to substance abuse to feel better about themselves and fit in with the crowd. However, if there is a serious substance abuse issue, it needs to be managed before a child can start learning how to achieve. The earlier an underachiever is identified, the sooner strategies can be put in place to help them achieve. And you will know you need to be vigilant. It is important to educate yourself for signs of substance abuse and then nip it in the bud.

Getting to the Root of the Problem

There can be many reasons for a child being an underachiever. I have always believed it was important to get to the root cause of a problem. Many professionals point to video games as the reason. From my experience, it is a symptom, not a cause. No doubt if a child spent the amount of time on studying that he does playing video games, he would do much better in school. You don't solve a problem by treating a symptom.

When evaluating your child, first look at family patterns. Mike had a weakness in verbal skills but was strong in math and science. Both his father and paternal grandfather were engineers. It made sense he was right-brained, like most engineers. In fact, when Mike studied engineering in college, he excelled.

If your child is adopted, you will not have family patterns to evaluate. But you may have some knowledge of your child's background. If your child is an international adoptee, then you have a different culture to consider. What are people from that culture known for? Do they have certain strengths?

One of the best ways to discover why your child is not doing well in school is to ask him. This may sound obvious but often, we don't do it. A technique called reflection can be very helpful. For instance, if your child brings home a poor grade on a test, don't tell him he didn't study enough. Sit him down and have a conversation, using reflection. Ask questions such as: Why do you think you did so poorly on the test? Do you think you do better on multiple-choice tests or essays? Why? Did you understand all the homework? Did you do all the homework? I think you can see where I am going with this. You may not get a lot of answers at first. But if you continue this practice, your child will begin to open up and you will be able to get a glimpse of what is not working for him. This information will be critical in helping to develop the right plan of action for his academic success. The reflection technique also helps someone solve their own problems and see the solutions. Now he can take ownership of his issues.

High School—Off to a Good Start

We all know that high school is when everything really begins to "count." A student's academic record as well as various activities and achievements will be the "currency" that gets him into a college of his choice. Of course, all the earlier educational years were important, too, as they established a foundation for learning, or possibly not in the case of an underachiever. Or, like my son Dave, they may have learned but not yet performed. Regardless, you have now arrived at the crossroads between middle school and high school. This is a time to take an objective look at your child and evaluate his strengths and weaknesses. Try to separate what you can change vs. what you cannot change and what you can control vs. what you cannot control. This will help you focus on the areas you can most impact to insure your child has a successful high school experience. believe there are several steps parents can easily take to help them make appropriate changes for their child.

First and foremost is testing. It will give you a snapshot of your child's strengths and weaknesses from which you can develop a plan.

Second, if your child qualifies, develop a 504 Plan to give him the accommodations he needs to level the playing field (a 504 Plan refers to a section of the Rehabilitation Act that allows accommodations and modifications to individuals with disabilities, so they can have a level playing field on which to compete with peers).

Third, you can retain an Educational Consultant who can help you develop a 504 Plan to keep your son on track throughout the school year.

Fourth, determine which high school would be the best fit for your child. Not all are created equal. Private schools offer niche opportunities.

Fifth, class placement to ensure that your child is placed in appropriate classes. This is a mistake we made with both of our sons. Plan with the goal in mind. A low start in math does not get a student to calculus by senior year.

Sixth, arrange for your son to be placed in an academic assistance class. If it is run well, this support will be key to his future success.

Seventh, hire a good tutor. She/he will be invaluable. Not only will a tutor help keep homework on track, but a tutor will also be a cheerleader for your son. An underachiever needs a team of people on his or her side rooting for him or her.

Eighth, activities can help bolster your child's confidence and may even be a key to college success.

Ninth, parental support and guidance are always most important. Your child really needs you to help him/her get past pitfalls and navigate the road to success.

Now, let's take a look at each of these items separately.

Testing

Psychological testing is probably one of the most important things you can do to prepare your child for high school. Most schools can provide testing but may only be willing to offer certain tests they think are necessary. I recommend having a private psychologist perform a complete battery of tests; even though it may be costly, it will be worth it.

Private testing is helpful for several reasons. First, you want a psychologist who is responsible to you and your child, not the school administration. Second, you want a complete set of tests and a detailed report explaining the results. Third, a psychologist can place the results in perspective for you and help you devise with an educational plan.

Once you have the test results, it will provide several pieces of important information. It will reveal your child's strengths and weakness. It will identify any learning disabilities. It will give you information you can use to help your child learn best. Being armed with this information will help you better guide your child through high school and into college.

If you do uncover a learning disability, this is a key piece of information. My sons both have ADHD, which qualified them for a 504 plan. A 504 plan allows accommodations in classes for students with certain learning disabilities. This can make a difference in their learning experience. My sons had accommodations that included preferential seating in the front of the class, repeating instructions on tests and assignments, and checking assignment books. Some students receive extra time on tests. Others are can have deadlines extended on assignments. Some students are given the chance to orally defend a test on which they performed poorly. As you can see, there are many different types of accommodations. If your child qualifies for one, it may be the difference between success and failure.

Which High School

Just as a good fit is important for college, it is probably even more important for high school because your child's future will be affected by the outcome. It is always important to remember that college choices will be related to high school performance.

After spending years in our highly regarded public school system, I had reservations about sending Mike there for high school. My plan had always been to send him to a single-sex Catholic high school nearby, which has a great reputation. I thought he would thrive in the all-boys environment. In fact, I heard Dr. Leonard Sax discuss single-sex schools and how they often benefit a child because they can use teaching strategies specific to either boys or girls. My experience has been that two-gender schools tend to favor girls and teachers often prefer them since their skill sets are suited to classroom learning. Unfortunately, my plan did not even get a fair hearing from my eighth-grade son who even refused to go to an Open House. He was so attached to his lifelong friends that he just couldn't bear the thought of leaving them. What I learned from this was that the planning process needs to start much earlier when you still have a lot of control over your child. If I wanted him to go to another high school, I probably should have moved him out of our school system around sixth grade. Then the transition to a new high school would not have met with much resistance especially if his school ended in eighth grade. A little strategic planning would have really helped in this situation. I had no idea how difficult a change would be until it was too late to make it. Even so, we always need to be aware of new windows of opportunity.

Sometimes you think the high school will be a good fit and then you find after a year or two, it is not working for your child. I had this happen with Mike at the end of his freshman year. That is when I contacted an educational consultant to help find the right school. After assessing the situation, he felt Mike could succeed at our public high school with the right support. After that, it was too late to move him. However, I have known boys who have moved schools later in high school. Usually they realize their situation and want to do it. Some may move after junior year and repeat junior year at the new school. I think that is a smart option since it gives the child extra time to mature as well as two years in a consistent environment. If a child is involved in sports and the school offers a better opportunity than where he/she is, it will be much easier to get his/her buy in.

I know you are probably thinking all this sounds good, but it comes with a hefty price tag. If your child is currently in public school, then the cost of a private school may strain your budget. It is important to always keep the goal in mind. It is much easier to get a child to change when they are younger rather than older. If he/she does not go to a high school where they can succeed, he or she may not succeed in college. Each step on the path is important and even more so when dealing with an underachiever. The one who navigates well will win.

High School Course Placement

At the end of eighth grade, your child will be recommended for a certain placement level in courses such as English, foreign language, math and science. This is something you need to take time to consider, especially if your child will not make it up to calculus in senior year. We had that problem with our son, Dave. Unfortunately, when he was finishing eighth grade, he was not doing well so we just went along with the recommendation, even though we knew his potential. This is where testing can help you. We knew he was in the 98th percentile for math. However, his performance always lagged, due to homework. Dave was recommended for a standard math class for freshman year. By sophomore year, he was doing better so we had him moved into honors math. However, with the low start at freshman year, he only made it to pre-calculus senior year. The result was that he could not take AP chemistry, which required calculus as a prerequisite. Consequently, Dave's high school transcript listed no AP classes. He was now a student on the rise, making the honor roll and receiving high scores on the ACT and SAT exams. But due to the lack of APs, we were concerned he would not be competitive in the college process. Fortunately, he was accepted at some very good colleges, mostly state universities. Even though he was courted by Columbia because of a high ACT score, he could not be competitive with its pool of applicants. Top colleges want to see APs on a transcript.

If your child should be in a similar situation, I recommend you try to find a math course at a local college that would be acceptable. He could repeat the course over the summer to be prepared to enter the next level.

Mike was in a different situation near the end of eighth grade. He had been recommended for both math and science honors as well as Spanish 3. That was in March. By April, he was declining and continued to slip through the end of the year. I was concerned he was not ready to handle the demands of high school, especially honors classes. Both his eighth grade and high school counselors offered little guidance. We decided Mike should start in regular classes until he demonstrated the ability to succeed. In many ways, I regret that decision. I think it sent a message to him that he is not smart. Teachers I have talked to about this have said that a child belongs at his level, even if he is not ready to embrace it. Looking back, I think I should have let him choose one honors class and then moved him into another one once he proved himself. Fortunately, kids are resilient. Mike is now a civil engineer with a large construction firm in the Washington, DC, area.

Educational Consultant

An educational consultant can be a useful resource when planning for high school or college. First, if your child needs testing, they can refer you to a good psychologist. Second, they can help you evaluate your public high school to determine if it is a good fit for your child. If not, based on your child's test results and personality, they can conduct a search and recommend other schools. Third, if your child needs a 504 Plan for accommodations, they can help arrange for this. In fact, before we requested accommodations for my son, Mike, the consultant was able to obtain a list of all the accommodations our high school had granted other students. This meant administrators would be more likely to accept the accommodations we requested. You can use an educational consultant as much or little as you choose, especially since you are paying for it. They are a helpful resource and can offer considerable support. Our educational consultant often attended teacher meetings with us. He was especially good with Mike because he was always so positive and hopeful for his future. It was important to have Mike hear uplifting words from another adult, especially one in the education field.

Tutor

A tutor can be a valuable addition to your resource team. A strong tutor will not only help a child tackle difficult homework assignments but will also help the child stay on task by teaching to check teacher websites and record assignments in his or her notebook. Dave worked with a wonderful tutor, Donna, who really made a difference in his academic life. Not only did she help him with homework, but she also served as a mentor. She believed in Dave's academic potential and helped to inspire him. She was primarily a tutor for writing projects and, through that process, she took Dave's natural gifts and developed them into a talent. During the college application process, she also worked with him to produce a quality essay. I also think Dave developed more discipline and a work ethic through a biweekly commitment to his tutor. He felt more accountable because he was in a one-on-one relationship with someone he respected and who appreciated him.

Sometimes a child just needs a tutor for a short period of time to get caught up in a subject if they have missed class time or needs individual help with key concepts. A tutor was also key to my daughter Brenda's success in AP calculus. If she had received a low grade in that class, she may not have been admitted to her first-choice college, even though she was a rowing recruit. Ivy League colleges require sports recruits to meet high academic standards along with their academic admits. Our one problem was finding a high-level math tutor. Brenda did not want to work with her teacher outside of class. This, of course, would have been too simple a solution. Our school did not have any other calculus tutors on its reference list. So, I did a lot of searching on the web and networking with other parents. Finally, I found one who teaches at a private school in our area through a source I had found online. Many teachers supplement their income through tutoring. If you are ever in desperate need of a tutor for your child like I was, I recommend that you call all the schools in your area for references. This may be the quickest and best way to get the right help for your child.

Academic Assistance

Most high schools have some form of academic assistance. Our high school had a course that taught study skills and had a professional who supervised and helped with homework.

This worked well for my younger son because he began the program in his freshman year. Through the years he was involved in the program, he developed a good rapport with an instructor, Emma. She wrote one of his college recommendations and I think the long-term relationship she had with Dave gave her a lot of prospective on his abilities. Emma also helped Dave raise expectations of himself. She always told him how capable he was. Eventually, he started believing it and began to soar. During a recent holiday break, Dave went to see her. Obviously, he had developed a strong bond with her.

On the other hand, my older son, Mike, did not want to be in an academic assistance class. He said it was for losers and he didn't consider himself to be one. So, he started freshman year without the extra help. Our educational consultant insisted that Mike enroll in the class in sophomore year. My boys are four years apart in school. When Mike was in the class, it was not very structured and was managed by a young woman right out of grad school. I do not think he benefited from the academic assistance class the way Dave had. After these experiences, my recommendation would be to study and analyze the program thoroughly to determine if it is a good fit for your child. Pay close attention to the person managing it.

It may be better to consider the extra help teachers and schools have in place during free periods. In some high schools, there are always teacher stations available in every subject that can be used during lunch or a free period. Many teachers offer assistance before and after class time to help struggling students. Some also have a period available during the day that may work if your child also has a free period that coincides. Remember, a child's teacher will always perceive a student favorably and give them the benefit of the doubt if he or she is trying to improve. This is the real bonus of working directly with a teacher.

504 Plan

A 504 Plan refers to a section of the Rehabilitation Act that allows accommodations and modifications to individuals with disabilities, so they can have a level playing field on which to compete with peers. Believe it or not, throughout the many years I participated in Planning and Placement Team meetings (PPTs) for my sons, I never heard any school professional mention the need for them to have a 504 plan. I only learned about a 504 Plan when I had both boys tested later in school. By that time, my older son had already finished his freshman year in high school. ADD qualifies a child for a 504 Plan. My boys had accommodations, which included preferential seating, repeating instructions, checking the assignment book, extra time to complete assignments, etc. There are many learning problems, as well as physical problems that will qualify a child for accommodations. It is really important that any child with a disability has a 504 Plan to help him achieve success in school. This is why psychological testing can be key. Through testing, a disability will be identified. Strengths will also be identified, which can be used to devise a plan for success.

One word of caution on a 504 Plan: You must remain vigilant to ensure it is being honored by teachers. A 504 Plan does not have the legal enforcement that an IEP (Individual Education Plan) has, thus teachers may treat it more casually. It is important to speak with each teacher prior to starting the school year to ensure they know your child has a 504 Plan and what it requires. Reminders throughout the year will help ensure your child is receiving the accommodations he is entitled to.

Parental Support

Parental involvement is key to success in school. Very few high achievers have done it alone. If you look at ethnic groups that are really successful academically, Jews and Asians come to mind, you will see parents who use their resources to support their children. We are in a school system with a large Jewish population. I have learned a lot from Jewish parents when it comes to managing my children's education. They are very involved and make sure their child gets whatever he needs at each stage to succeed. They also push for more homework and summer enrichment requirements. Homework also develops discipline and a strong work ethic. This has enabled my daughter, Brenda, to succeed. As a collegiate rower, she has many demands on her schedule. But throughout her years in our school system, she developed a lot of discipline and a strong work ethic.

I know our sons would not have fared as well in school without our involvement. We always tried to stay on top of whatever problem they had. Fortunately, we also had financial resources to help resolve the problem. But it is not only about finances. You must manage your child. You have to ensure he or she is doing homework and knows how to check assignments using a teacher website or an assignment book. You may have to help your child with his homework. In high school especially, you need to manage how your child is spending time and with whom. The last thing you want is for your child to slip into behaviors that will be difficult to reverse. Many people think once a child is in late middle school, they can be left on their own. Not so. This is the time for extreme vigilance. It is not only school work you need to monitor, but also lifestyle choices. Keeping a child busy with constructive activities can help limit the amount of available free time. This might all sound like a lot of work but the time you dedicate now will mean you will have free time later. I devote a tremendous amount of time and sacrificed a lot of my personal life, but I now have peace of mind knowing my boys are independent and achieving success.

Activities

It is important for an underachiever to be involved in an activity whether it be a team sport, individual sport, scouting, music, the arts, or something else. Successful participation in an activity can raise a child's self-esteem. It provides an opportunity to have an adult mentor and positive peer group. It teaches the connection between hard work and success and the importance of goal setting. My son, Mike, loved team sports. He gained a lot of self-esteem testing his skills against other boys his age. If he hadn't wanted to continue playing football, I'm not sure we could have convinced him to attend college. My younger son, Dave, never did well in team sports. One day, we noticed how fit our neighbor Greg had become and how much happier he seemed to be. It turned out he had been boxing. We enrolled Dave in a boxing program, too. He was able to work out on his own time and terms, and the act of hitting a boxing bag relieved much of his stress. The boxing club owner, an immigrant from Latin America, was an unlikely mentor. However, Rodrigo accepted boys as they were. Whenever he talked to Dave, he never failed to use uplifting words. Once, Dave told me Rodrigo asked him what college sport he wanted to play. The notion that someone thought he could play a college sport raised Dave's expectations of himself. Both of my sons also were Boy Scouts and I am proud to be a mother of two Eagle Scouts. One thing I love about the scouting program is that it teaches boys how to reach a goal through a step-by-step approach. Teachers call this approach chunking. I guess they learned from Boy Scouts that it works. Boy Scouts also provides a positive environment with adult mentors and older male role models. The program can have a powerful effect on a boy. My son Mike also played in the high school band. Once I realized a lot of successful students were in band, I kept Mike in the program through high school so he would be part of a positive peer group. The band teacher was also a great role model and a positive mentor. As you may have noticed, I discuss peer group and adult mentors a lot. Since Mike chose friends who were mostly underachievers like himself, I thought it was important for him to have other types of peer groups to provide a different type of influence. Adult mentors are important. An underachiever rarely receives positive feedback from teachers. They often get it from an adult who is involved in their activity. Words are powerful. They have the power to set positive change in motion. A child often disregards the compliments given by his parents because he feels they are not objective and just want to be kind. But when another adult he respects praises him or her, it can go a long way to building confidence.

Tactics to Consider

Three tactics can help turn an underachiever around: (1) the cultivation of self-discipline, (2) a study space free of distractions and incentives/rewards that can be used to motivate right action, and (3) celebrate accomplishments.

Self-Discipline

Self-discipline is one of the most important traits a person can possess for success. But even if someone doesn't have it, self-discipline can be cultivated. By developing a plan, setting priorities and developing systems and routines, self-discipline can be acquired. Of course, self-discipline can often be learned first through other activities before it is applied to academics. This is one of the benefits of sports. Self-discipline is learned by showing up on time and practicing skills. Through the game or competition, a child learns the connection between practice and performance. To establish self-discipline, I recommend using one of your child's interests for an activity. It could be sports, music, or something else as long as your child understands the relationship between practice and performance.

Study Space

An isolated study space such as a "study bubble" is essential to academic success especially for an underachiever. You may be wondering what is a study bubble. When my son, Mike, went to college, they had them on every floor of his dorm and also other places on campus. Basically, it was a glass-enclosed study area for one person's use. During his freshman year, Mike used the study bubble on occasion. During his sophomore year, it became an effective habit and he found it helped him focus so he could better concentrate on his studies. I credit the study bubble for helping him make the Dean's List that fall. Some underachievers, especially those with ADD or other learning disabilities, need a place free of distractions in order to study. This also may be helpful at home. Most kids' rooms are distracting—I know my kids' rooms were—and one of the worst places for them to do homework. Oftentimes, I had them work in the dining room or another location in the house. We have a home office with a computer so that was also better than their bedrooms. If our town library had been open in the evenings, I would have taken my boys there. You may have a library open at night. If so, it may help to have them develop study habits that include library time while they are young, so it will be natural when they are in college. Let's face it, a dorm room is usually the last place anyone can concentrate. Habits that are honed at home will likely continue into college life and beyond.

Use Incentives/Rewards

Some kids respond to incentives and rewards. This may just be what they need to get motivated. When children are young, simple rewards can work well. When they are older, they may need something more significant to get motivated. Once when we wanted Mike to perform, we put up a chart with a picture of the prize at the end. He had one month to win the prize. At first, he resisted. But as time was running out, his desire for the prize grew. Finally, on nearly the last day he performed and won the prize. The older the child, the harder it may be to get results, especially if he is, resistant. I recommend creating incentives for shorter, more achievable goals first. It could be something like getting all the homework done within the week. The next goal might be to study a certain amount of time for the test. Obviously, it would be wonderful if your child earned an A. But the important thing is to begin developing the right habits—process over product. Eventually, the "A" will come. And you don't want an underachiever to get discouraged because all the work didn't produce an "A" the first time. Eventually, when your student is more confident, you may want to associate a prize with a grade on the test. This may motivate your child in the classroom. One caution, while rewards provide a positive incentive, punishments often increase resistance. Once a child—particularly a teen—becomes resistant, it takes much more work to change the behavior. I have found it best not to bring it out in the first place.

Not Ready for Prime Time—Students on the Decline

Let's face it, there are some students who are just not ready for the next step, whether it be in high school or onto college. They are in an underachiever mode for whatever reason. Most of the reasons were addressed earlier. My son Mike was in this position. He was not handling the demands of our high school. We considered finding a private school for him to attend and contacted an educational consultant to help us do that. This was the only open window we had to change during the high school years. Of course, I had some concerns about it—especially sending him to a boarding school where he may not have the supervision he had at home. The peer group would become even more powerful at a boarding school. That's fine if it is a positive peer group. However, if it's not, our son could have ended up with bigger problems. The educational consultant mentioned a couple of private boarding schools, which I did not feel were appropriate. He primarily persuaded us to let Mike remain at our high school and retain him to help Mike make it through. So, that is what we did. However, there are also other options to consider, such as home school and other state high schools. We entertained these options for our younger son Dave but realized they were not the best for him. Some kids who are not doing well in high school even opt to finish at a night school set up for that purpose. Next, let's take a more in-depth look at these options for students on the decline in high school.

Home School

Sometimes high school is not working for a student and parents consider homeschooling. This was an option I considered for Dave but ruled it out because I felt he needed the socialization. However, I have seen a lot of home schooling success stories. And there are now many resources to support you. There are home schooling groups that meet to support each other. They also plan outings so the kids can interact with peers. There are also various home school curricula online. Parents do not need to do all the teaching anymore. Recently, I learned about a home school co-op. Several families banned together and rented space for the home school. They also hired teachers for certain subjects, such as physics and orchestra. From what I've heard, this arrangement is working very well. One boy I know who attends the school has thrived and is applying to top colleges. The home school co-op has developed him into a confident and competent learner.

Night School

I recently learned that several high schools in our area participate in a night school program for struggling students. These students attend school four nights a week, Monday through Thursday. During the day, they are encouraged to have a job to gain work experience. Work experience is designed to give them responsibility and discipline. They have an opportunity to learn some practical skills. It also gives them a glimpse at what type of work they would be qualified to do without an education or training. Sometimes underachievers just need a good reality check to get motivated. Mike certainly did. While he never went the night school route, he learned some equally life-changing lessons during his postgraduate year. Having grown up in a wealthy community, he did not have much contact with people who were different than himself. During his 13th year, he encountered students who, he said, "didn't use their brain nor did they even have one." I think he realized then how important it was to be an educated person with a sharp, well-trained brain. Regarding night school, the mom I talked to about it said it was working effectively for her son. He would also receive his degree from his regular high school, a highly regarded one. I think for certain students this could be the best way to finish high school. This is certainly better than dropping out and having to earn a GED. Passing that test is not easy. Most home-schooled students need to take a prep course to insure they succeed. The GED test is about seven hours long and must be passed with a 70% of what high school students would earn on the test. Night school is certainly a better alternative to achieve a high school degree.

Special State High Schools

Another group of schools you may want to consider are the special state schools. Our state has a variety of special high schools that residents can attend. Some of them are magnet schools for students who excel in subjects such as science. Others are for students with special talents such as theatre arts. In addition, there are various technical high schools that offer to train students in a trade—anything from plumbing to hair dressing. However, I discovered there are a variety of high schools in our state quite by accident. I had called the State Education Department with a question. During our conversation, the administrator told me about the various high schools and even emailed the list. I was especially interested in the aquaculture school for Dave. The one that was closest would also allow him to attend his home high school half of the day. I also learned that the school district has to designate its involvement with a school. If a school isn't already included, I was told it would not be difficult to get one approved. State high schools can offer a good alternative for some students. And the best thing about them is they are free to taxpayers if you qualify. If you are not satisfied with your high school, it would be worthwhile looking into what other options your state offers. I suggest you contact your State Department of Education. If a school may be of interest to you and your child, then you should contact your school district. If you are meeting with roadblocks, I recommend seeking out an educational consultant to help you. While consultants charge a fee, they will save you time and get the best possible result for your child.

Out-of-District Schools

Another option most people are not aware of is that an out-of-district student may be able to get into another school system if space is available. This requires out-of-district tuition but if the school is a better fit, it may be worth it. This option works especially well if a student needs a fifth year of high school to earn credits for graduation. This frees the student from the social stigma of repeating a year at a sensitive time in his life. Frequently, the home high school is more than happy to cooperate and send their challenged student off for another school system to be managed. So, you will probably find a lot of support amongst administrators for this strategy.

Private Schools

Private high schools can be a good alternative. Our educational consultant was familiar with those in our area and suggested a couple of options that could work well for our son. The best one, in his opinion, required boarding—something we did not want. We felt our son would be better served by remaining at home. If you want to consider private schools, I would consider a consultant who is familiar with them. Of course, you can also do all the work yourself which is quite time consuming. And of course ask questions of your child's school counselor and other parents who may be struggling with the same issues. Networking with other parents can often be very useful.

Students on the Decline— Post-High School Options

Some students make it through high school only to discover they are not ready for college or have not prepared themselves to be competitive in the college process. Mike fell into this category. It was helpful he believed he needed to wait before attending college. He chose to do a postgraduate year at a school dedicated only to that one year between high school and college.

The all-male school also helps prepare boys for the rigors of college sports. Football was Mike's driving force. He wanted to play in college but realized he needed more development since his high school experience had been lacking. Mike could have taken some other routes as well such as community college, a local college or university, or a Gap Year program. Depending on your goals for your child and their own preferences, one of these paths might work well for them.

Community College

Community College may be a good choice for some underachievers or those who do not have the financial means to attend a four-year university right away. Community colleges in California, for instance, are part of the University of California (UC) college system. My friend's son attended his local community college and then as a junior, transferred to UC Berkeley where he received a BA degree. Berkeley, like most UC universities, has a competitive admissions process. He may not have been accepted to Berkeley as a freshman. By attending a community college, he was able to earn two years of college credit, save money, and transfer to one of the top universities in the country. A UC Berkeley degree on a resume will always have substantial value.

Another boy, Sam, ended up attending our local community college after dropping out of a four-year college due to illness. He had to return home for treatment, so it made sense for him to continue earning college credit locally. One day, I saw his father, who told me that Sam was finally achieving academic success. The effect it was having on him was transformative. Sam remained at the community college for two years. During that time, one of our local universities started a new program in his major. Sam is currently at that university continuing to thrive in the area of his strengths.

I briefly considered community college for my son Mike. However, I believe several issues must be considered before making this decision. Fortunately, I had been taking a class at the community college so I had a firsthand look at the college accounting for Mike's strengths, weaknesses, and personality. I did not think this college would achieve what I wanted for him. I was especially concerned it would not inspire him to continue to a four-year college or university because it did not have the vibrancy of a traditional college campus. It also didn't have a football team, so he would not have been able to play the sport he loved. And most of the students did not appear to be the peer group I thought would help set the bar high. Again, I evaluated this option against who my son is. While I did not think this community college was a good option for him, it certainly worked quite well for our friend Sam. As the saying goes, different strokes for different folks. If Mike had not gone to a postgraduate (PG) school, I would have considered a four-year university in our area where he could have taken classes.

Local College or University

We have several universities in our area that would have enabled Mike to attend classes and commute from home. For him, I felt this might have been a better option than a community college because he would have had the chance to experience a real college environment. He would have met students who were motivated and, hopefully, motivating, and he would have been able to test himself with college level classes without the commitment of a full workload. Recently, I took a course at one of our local universities, so I had a chance to evaluate it against the local community college. I was impressed with the variety of activities and the intellectual curiosity of the students. I thought Mike would have been inspired if he had attended classes there. One important thing I learned was that this university will allow students who take a prescribed number of classes and earn a certain GPA to matriculate. This was certainly a well-kept secret—something I learned through talking with friends. That is why it is so important to reach out to people. Don't depend solely on your child's high school counselor or even an educational consultant. No one knows everything about all available options for this type of student. This was the route my son's friend, Ben, would follow. After leaving his first college, Ben's parents enrolled him in classes at the local university. Unfortunately, at the end of each semester, he did not have the GPA to matriculate. However, there was and is always another option. Currently, he is taking classes at the University of Connecticut-Stamford. He is also pursuing a plumbing apprenticeship. This is one of the benefits of taking a lighter college curriculum, even though it may take longer to obtain a degree. For Ben, he will emerge from this process with a bachelor's degree and a solid trade skill. That just might be his path to success.

The Thirteenth Year

Gap Year. Today, the gap year has become an acceptable alternative to immediate entrance into college. And there are all sorts of programs being offered. It is both important to know your child and your goals for your child. Start with your end goal in mind. Some gap year options could really backfire. I knew one boy who decided to spend a year traveling abroad. Four years later, he is still traveling, working odd jobs on occasion, and being supported mostly by his parents. A gap year varies with each individual child; some students are able to take a gap year for a cultural experience and then move on to college the following year.

Post-Graduate School. We knew Mike needed a safe place to mature where he could also gain confidence as a student. A postgraduate year, which many private schools offer, seemed to be the best choice. However, it requires a student to be a fifth-year senior and fit in with the students who have already been there for three years and know the ropes. We felt this may not be a good situation for Mike since he would not be on an equal playing field. If we had looked further, we might have been able to sort through the myriad schools to find the one that would give him the best chance of success. But we chose instead to explore a one-year postgraduate program for boys. The school also emphasized sports, which was attractive to Mike since he wanted to better develop himself for college football.

The postgraduate school proved to be the right choice for Mike. Its structured approach provided a suitable environment for developing the discipline and work ethic important for academic success. The academics were at a level that enabled Mike to succeed and gain confidence, which was important for him. At our extremely competitive high school, Mike had been beaten down. He needed to realize how smart he is and that with hard work, he would be competitive. Mike earned high honors during his first semester. What a boost to his self-esteem that was! In addition to academics, Mike also received first-rate training from the football coach. Consequently, the college head football coach came to the school to recruit Mike and another player. They both enrolled in the university. Not only that, but they were also roommates during freshman year. This eliminated "roommate risk," which can interfere with college adjustment.

A PG (postgraduate) year is certainly not a miracle cure. Mike's college freshman year was still a nail bitter—but he did stay out of academic trouble as he learned how to function in a college environment. By sophomore year, he had figured it out and made the Dean's List in engineering.

As I reflect on all this, I think it was important to give him the gift of time. In fact, I have noticed a lot of growth in boys between ages 18 and 19. In Mike's case, the gift of time needed to be coupled with a boost in confidence as a learner. He required an academic environment where he could be successful.

One important fact I learned about the PG year is that colleges have various views about it. Some will consider it a fifth-year and average the grades into the student's high school GPA. This is what you hope will happen when you have had a high school underachiever. However, some colleges just look at it as a gap year and consider the experience—how you chose to spend your time. In this case, your high school records stand alone. We were disappointed when one of Mike's top choices took this position, especially since we had such high hopes in a "college that changes lives." Regardless, Mike ended up at a university that changed his life. Besides making the Dean's List, Mike has been named to the ODAC (Old Dominion Athletic Conference) Academic Team and received ODAC honors in his position as defensive end. We couldn't be more pleased with the positive impact this university had on Mike.

Small Steps for Gaining Momentum

Small steps in the right direction will build momentum over time. Never underestimate the power of small steps. In fact, you probably will not be able to get your child moving forward in any other way. When Mike started struggling in high school, my husband wanted him to immediately rise above his challenges. This doesn't work. Most people, you and I included, cannot change that quickly. I like to think about how I climbed some mountains in the Alps. It was only by putting one foot in front of the other again and again over time, that I finally reached the Swiss Alpine Hut at the top. This is what I had to do with Mike to help him. I even told his counselor and teachers that I was not seeking overnight success. All I wanted was to gently nudge him in the right direction a few degrees at a time. Apparently, this is how a huge tanker ship also gets turned. Eventually, those small steps develop momentum as confidence building leads to success. With a bit of patience, Mike made the necessary changes to succeed; it is how he made the Dean's List in engineering at his college. With small steps, he was also learning that success is achieved with small acts daily. Success is not a sprint—it is a long-distance run where a work ethic and training make all the difference.

Students on the Rise

Pygmalion Effect/What Helped Turn Dave Around

If you have ever seen *My Fair Lady*, then you know something about the Pygmalion effect. Basically, it is what happens to someone when you raise their expectations through praise or belief in themselves. I read about a study where a random group of students were labeled as gifted, thus setting teachers' expectations high. During the course of the program, these students proved they were indeed gifted by meeting all of the expectations of the course curriculum. But, in reality, they were a varied group of learners with only a few gifted students among them. This demonstrates what can happen when expectations are raised.

Dave was turned around, in part, by the Pygmalion effect. One of his teachers, who had taught the gifted, wrote on his paper, "I like how you think." Coming from her, it was a true compliment and made him realize someone appreciated his brain. At the same time, he also had an academic support teacher who told him how capable he was. The combination of a meaningful compliment and high expectations helped Dave start believing in himself. I also think this happened at a time in his maturity when he was able to seize upon it and succeed. Dave began taking his studies, and especially his homework, more seriously. This led him to making the Honor Roll and becoming a "student on the rise" who was able to compete well in the college admissions process. Colleges do recognize some students are immature and take a while to grow. Thus, a student on the rise is well regarded. Due to his scholastic improvement, Dave was able to move into honors classes, which helped strengthen his academic schedule. Not only was Dave accepted into most of the colleges to which he applied, but he was also invited into the College Park Scholars program, a theme-based honors program. The success he achieved through the Pygmalion effect was convincing.

I recommend you seek teachers and adult mentors who can offer your child a meaningful compliment, along with high expectations. This simple approach can have a tremendous impact. It can change a child from an underachiever to one whose life reflects success.

Power of Maturity

There is nothing like maturity. In my experience, it does resolve a lot of the problems. When a child is not mature, he or she does not have the ability to understand the reasons behind the requirements. Frequently, it is not just emotional immaturity—it is actual brain immaturity. Some brains just take longer to mature, especially if there are learning disabilities involved. I found everything so much easier when my child had actually reached the level of maturity required to function successfully. But how do we handle an immature child when they are expected to work at a level beyond their development? The answer is we need to give them a lot of support and help fill in the blanks. By that I mean, if your child does not have the executive functioning skills to plan and organize their work, then you may need to sit down and assist them in doing that. But don't expect he or she will be able to solo the next time. Repetition does help. But much still depends on maturity. And some people may never be able to do it well. Take my husband, for instance, who suffers from adult ADD. He was very excited when he bought a Blackberry. He thought it would be the answer to all his organizational problems. Unfortunately, about half the time he forgets to enter the information into his Blackberry so it can keep him on track. He did not get the early training my boys received. Today, that training combined with their maturity is contributing to success. It only took until they were 19-20 years old. Thus, don't expect immediate results. Parents of children who mature more slowly need to be long-distance runners, not sprinters. The goal line is in the distance and we will get there by putting one foot in front of the other over a long period of time. I only learned this at the end. No one ever told me it would take so long. I expected results much sooner. Anyone who tells you a workshop is the answer does not know the entire story. It is still important to enroll your child in workshops that can help with study skills, but results won't be immediate. However, I do believe they retain a lot of what they have learned and will be able to tap into it when they are ready. It is all a process. The key is to continue moving forward the best you can.

Getting Support Important

An underachiever will need support along the way to become successful. It is up to you as the parent to keep a watchful eye on your child's academics. There is no shame in getting help. At one point, Dave needed extra help for math. He wasn't able to find the time to meet with his regular teacher. Fortunately, the year before, I had found a high-level math teacher for my daughter, so I was able to locate a resource right away. However, it isn't always easy to find a resource. I found a math tutor through an online search, then followed up on recommendations. As it turned out, he was a teacher at a local private school. I have learned many private school teachers tutor on the side to earn extra money. I highly recommend you call the private schools in your area. Your guidance office may also have a list of tutors. Remember, not all tutors are created equal. So, you should interview them and check references before hiring. You definitely do not want a tutor to backfire with your child. Finding an appropriate tutor will be invaluable. You may need to rely on a tutor several times during the high school years. When dealing with an underachiever, a parent must have a support team. This includes an educational consultant, tutors, a psychologist, and school guidance counselors. Not everyone will see the child the same way. Many times, I was able to gain insights into my sons through the various members of their support team. As a parent, this helped me to be a better guiding force because it is up to us to navigate the path toward college success for our child.

Increase Schedule Strength through Honors and Aps

It is important to increase a high school student's strength of schedule as they move along. This will help them create a "student on the rise" profile for colleges. He or she can strengthen their schedules by adding honors and/or AP classes. The difference between honors and AP classes is that a high school determines its own honors curriculum. AP classes are based on a national curriculum. At the end of a course, a test is given. Top colleges accept AP credit for scores in the 4- to 5-range. However, other colleges often accept credit for a 3 score. AP classes are especially important to top colleges because it shows how students perform within the same curriculum guidelines and test. AP credit can also help save on college tuition expenses.

Dave started out fairly low in high school freshman year. He was not recommended for any honors courses, so he took non-honors classes. By the end of the second semester, he had improved. We requested he be moved into math honors. That one increase started to add an upwardly mobile picture to his profile. In addition, honors classes at our school are weighted, meaning grades in those classes are worth more than in non-honors classes. If a student does well in an honors class, it can benefit his GPA. So, he/she will not only look like he/she is taking tougher courses, but his /her GPA will also improve at the same time. During junior year, we added science honors. Again, with grades weighted, Dave's GPA continued to climb quickly. He did so well in chemistry junior year, he wanted to take AP chemistry senior year. Unfortunately, our small high school did not offer it. And Dave could not qualify for AP physics since he was not in calculus, only pre-calculus. Math placement freshman year came back to haunt us senior year. Looking back, we should have made sure he received a math placement, which would have put him in calculus by senior year. Regardless, Dave's transcript reflected a student on the rise—something colleges appreciate. Admissions officers understand that many students are immature freshman year. Our educational consultant often said that colleges don't even consider freshman year. Who really knows for sure? But one thing we do know is that Dave fared well in the college process. He also had some good scores on the SAT and ACT to accompany his student-on-the-rise transcript. It helped that he kept increasing the strength of his schedule and performed well. As you can tell, we took baby steps. Even small steps get you there. Underachievers are more likely to perform well by taking one small step at a time. It certainly was true in Dave's case and I am sure it will also be true in your child's case. Small successes will lead to bigger successes.

Handling the College Application

The college application process is critical to your child's success. It is not something to leave to chance. Some parents hire an Educational Consultant who specializes in this. In our case, we did it ourselves because we were willing to dedicate ourselves to the required process and research it would take. It helped that my husband had been a local admissions counselor for a top university so he was familiar with the process and requirements. Because we were passionate about the importance of the process to our son, we put all our effort into finding the right schools. We used various means to do this, which are available to you at very a low cost.

College Search Resources

Naviance. This program lists colleges to which students from the high school are accepted. It will give you an idea if your child meets the criteria for acceptance. This is a good sorting tool because it says these colleges met a certain cultural litmus test for your child's peers.

Princeton Review and Other College Books. They give details that Naviance doesn't provide, but they list less than 400 colleges—although there are thousands to choose from.

US News Colleges. This is an electronic college reference that is inexpensive—I paid about $15 for several months access. If you combine all three of these resources into your search, you will have expert guidance.

There are also many other things you need to do to prepare. But don't worry. Most of these items will take place over a period of time so you can focus on them one at a time. By the time your child is ready to apply for college, you will have a plan in place to strengthen his or her academic schedule. Then you will have him do whatever is necessary to prepare for the SAT and ACT tests. If he /she will use sports to boost admission chances, they are already involved in a sports activity and working to develop as an athlete. College application time is the time to take stock of your child's strengths and weaknesses. There are many colleges that are niche-oriented. If your child has a special talent or strength, a niche college will allow him to succeed. There are numerous other points to consider when applying to college such as admission rates, rolling/priority applications, small colleges vs. large universities, semester grades, and whether or not to use an educational consultant. Now let's take a look at these points in more detail.

SAT and ACT Tests. These two tests are now accepted by most colleges in the US. It pays to investigate each test to determine which one would be most suitable for your child since they vary to some degree. Of course, it may be best to take both. But colleges will want to see both scores.

The regular SAT tests only reading and math skills, and also includes an essay. Scoring is done by subtracting the number of wrong answers from right answers. Guessing is not rewarded in this test unless the guess is correct. Students are best advised to skip questions to which they do not know the answer.

The ACT tests five areas: English, math, reading, science, and writing. Scoring is done by counting the number of right answers.

Many people consider the SAT test to be more of an IQ test while the ACT test focuses on what a student has learned. I have found there is some truth to that. Thus, a student who has applied himself in school may find an advantage with the ACT. If not, the SAT may be a better choice. The other difference between the tests is that the ACT has various subject areas. Often, colleges do not require SAT subject tests if a student submits the ACT score. However, a student who has a weakness in science, for instance, may prefer not to take that test. My son Dave benefitted from the ACT because he posted a top score in science, which probably helped him get accepted by a good engineering school.

I recommend spending time reviewing the SAT and ACT websites to learn more about the differences between the two tests. If you feel your child may do poorly on one of the tests, it is probably best not to take it since colleges will want to see the results. There is also an advantage to taking the same test more than once. Many colleges will use the top scores from multiple tests. For example, they will take the high math score from a March test along with the high verbal score from the October test. There are certain strategies involved with test taking, particularly for top students. In my opinion, underachievers are best served by not inflating the scores through a strategy of over prepping. Remember, you want your child to find a suitable college. If your child ends up in a college with a better name, more challenging academics, and stiffer competition, they may end up failing, if is not adequately prepared. Your goal is for your child to go to a college that will support them and help encourage success.

Educational Consultant for College

Educational Consultants definitely serve a purpose. As I mentioned previously, they can be a great resource for getting your child off to a good start in high school. However, I think they can have mixed results when it comes to the college process. No doubt, if you do not have the time to put into a thorough effort, an educational consultant is the way to go. Even just a consultation may be worthwhile since they have a great deal of experience with students, especially from your high school. They also seem to have good relationships with certain college admissions staff, so they are much more familiar with what that particular college's process is. And they have resources for essay help, SAT prep, and application preparation. However, I also think an educational consultant has limitations. They have their list of favorite colleges for students and they often do not venture beyond that. This was certainly the case with my son who ended up at a college that was a perfect fit, which our educational consultant had downplayed. I think there were two reasons for his feelings.

First, no one from our high school had attended this college in many years so it may have been perceived as a poor fit for our culture.

Second, he was not familiar with all the changes that had occurred over the years, which made it a viable choice for my son

No one really knows and loves a child like the parent. No educational consultant would have ever outperformed me for my child. I spent a lot of time researching colleges using various tools such as Naviance, US News College, and Princeton Review. I went on numerous websites to read about the colleges. I always read the Mission Statement and president's welcome first. That sets a tone that cannot be underestimated. Since Mike was also interested in playing football, I read about coaches and teams. I even used the D3football website as a resource. Actually, if a college wasn't on their list, it wasn't on Mike's. His college search was football driven. I doubt a college educational consultant would have understood the importance of that. I also accompanied Mike on most of his college visits, so I could witness his reaction to campuses, coaches, and what he heard at an information session. This was critical information because it helped focus the search on the right colleges. A parent will do this to some extent anyway. But when you are also your child's consultant, you view things from that perspective, too. I do not think an educational consultant could have done any better for my son than I did.

Going for Strengths

Focusing on strengths is what will make someone successful. High school is a time to develop a variety of academic skills and gain a core foundation of knowledge.

Some underachievers, like Mike, may have certain weaknesses that may make success in high school more difficult. Due to some LD (learning disability) issues, Mike was not much of a reader or writer and seriously lacked executive functioning skills. However, college is completely different from high school. Fortunately, he chose a college that had an engineering school. If it had not been for serendipity, he might have ended up at a small liberal arts college where language arts predominate. At an engineering school, Mike was able to get into the area of his strengths right away—math and science. This enabled him to immediately excel and ultimately succeed. I recommend helping your child find his areas of strength. Usually when they do, they find their passion.

Rolling/Priority Applications

A lot of colleges have rolling and/or priority applications. Priority applications are submitted by a certain early date—often by November 1 or December 1. These applications will be given a priority in terms of their review for admission. This can be important because colleges will not know by the early date what their full range of applications will look like. By applying early, a marginal student may have a better chance of admission. We used priority applications during Dave's college process every time we could. One of the biggest benefits of this was that by the end of January, he knew whether or not he had been accepted to his top college. As luck would have it, he was accepted so we could rest easy until the end of the school year. Believe me, senior year is anything but typical especially in a highly competitive high school where most of the students are using early decision and priority admissions, both of which require November 1 applications in most cases. The college process dominates most of the first semester. Those who are accepted into one of their preferred colleges, are relieved of stress as soon as that happens.

Many large universities and perhaps some smaller colleges also use rolling admissions. Under rolling admissions, colleges and universities are continually accepting students until they reach the maximum. This gives students an opportunity to decide to attend a four-year college much later in the process. It also enables them to apply to a college after they know where he or she has been accepted. There are some students whose college application list does not include a good mix of stretches, matches and, more importantly, safety schools. There have been some strong students at our high school who have been rejected from every college on their 12-college list. However, colleges with rolling and late admissions help these students by accepting them. Students should pay special attention to those that have high admit numbers—75% or above. A high admission number does not mean it is an inferior college. In fact, Mike had attended a college that had high admission numbers, which was a great fit for him and a well-respected regional college. Just keep in mind there are various strategies you can use to help your child gain acceptance to college.

Sports Recruitment

Sports recruitment can help in gaining acceptance to a college of your choice. My son, Mike, wanted to play football at the D-3 level. Most D-3 football teams are associated with small liberal arts colleges. It is easier than you might think to be a D-3 football recruit. One of the most important things to do is to go to the college's sports website and fill out the recruiting form. Mike was one of the most highly recruited on his football team even though he was not one of the most talented. The reason: I went on all the websites of his prospective colleges, which I found on d3football.com, and filled out the form. He was getting so many calls from coaches that he finally had to tell me to stop. For a kid who was tentative about college, this helped make him feel wanted and it boosted his confidence. Many liberal arts colleges have started football teams in an effort to attract more boys to campus. If a college has more than 60% of one gender, there is a drop-off of interest among both genders. Some colleges are starting football teams for just this reason. They know it is important to keep the right balance to attract students. I heard that one college football coach had to recruit 300 players just to get his yield for a 100-player team. If a college coach is willing to support a player, this support may help give him or her an edge for admission. In addition, while D-3 athletics do not allow sports scholarships, our son did get offered a number of academic scholarships. The college he chose gave him $9,000 per year for four years. I also had learned that getting a good match with a college team helps make the transition into college much smoother. Mike did not get off to the best start academically but because he played football, he was happy and persevered. There was also a huge benefit to having coaches and players involved with your child while trying to make the adjustment to college life. I found the older players helpful because they offered practical advice and provided role models. Mike got off to a great start because of his sports involvement and it continued to help him develop discipline and a work ethic as well as time management. On the D-3 level, I only have experience with football. My daughter was a D-1 recruit in rowing. When an athlete is at the D-1 level, they have some great opportunities including tuition-free college. My daughter wanted an Ivy League college, which doesn't offer scholarships. However, because she had strong grades and scores along with the coach's support, she was accepted. As a recruit, she applied early—in October—to one college only. However, one top university told her that if it didn't work out, they would have a couple of spaces in reserve that she could apply for. Brenda's team experience has been one of the best things about college. She made friends with everyone on her college men's and women's teams and she met other rowers throughout the country. She had an extensive network when she graduated.

Semester Grade Reporting

Your high school counselor will probably tell you that the school will be sending the first-semester grades of your senior year to all the colleges to which you applied. If you have strong semester grades, there should not be a problem. However, my daughter, Brenda, was an athletic recruit and her first college choice—like most Ivies—does not even like to see a grade below a B. Unfortunately, Brenda had a poor start on senior high school year since she missed classes for both college visits and illness. Her AP calculus class suffered. In fact, she was near failing when we hired a tutor to help her recover. By the end of the semester, she was just hoping the teacher's generosity would result in a C—but it was still not good enough to ensure she would be accepted by this Ivy League college. This was a dilemma made even more difficult because her senior year counselor was new to the school and did not have much experience with athletic and Ivy league applications or school protocol. Even if she had been a seasoned counselor, I am not sure she would have had a solution. Consequently, we scheduled a meeting with the head of the guidance office. If we did not formulate a plan, I do not think Brenda would have been accepted into her first-choice college. This is what we proposed to do. First, do not send first semester grades to the college—wait until they ask for them. Second, if asked for the grades, include the teacher's progress report on the next quarter, which hopefully will be an improvement. The head of guidance agreed to this proposal, as this was done before. As it turned out, the college never asked for first-semester grades. Brenda continued to work with the tutor and finished the year with an A in AP calculus. And she received a 5 on the AP exam, the highest score possible. My point in sharing this story is that every rule does not needs be followed. If something will be a problem, be proactive about it. It could mean the difference between admission and denial.

Admission Statistics

One of the first things everyone does when embarking on the college process is to look at college admission statistics. If a college accepts only 8% of its applicants, it will be difficult to gain admission. However, there are four doors to admission. The typical academic door, the legacy door, the athletic recruitment door, and the minority door. If you fit into one of those, like my daughter did, your chances of admittance go up astronomically. However, if a college accepts 80% of its applicants, most will meet with success.

Most high school counselors encourage students to have a list of colleges they plan to apply to ranging from safety to match to a stretch. Applicants use admission statistics as a key determining factor for their list. However, if they are only going by university admission at a large university, their calculations could be considerably flawed.

Dave's first choice for college admission was a large state university. The year he was applying, the admit rate was 40%. That number gave me much cause for concern. Dave was a student on the rise at a top high school, had taken some honors courses, and had relatively competitive ACT and SAT scores. However, he had not taken any AP courses. As with most large universities, a student applies to a particular school within that university. In Dave's case, it was the College of Engineering. Consequently, I spent a lot of time on the College of Engineering website which had numerous pages. It was easy to get lost in cyberland. Then one day, I stumbled upon the engineering admission rate—it was 72%--more than 30% higher than the university admit rate. I was overjoyed. It seemed nearly certain Dave would be accepted. And he was. Not only that, he was also invited into their theme-based honors program, a living learning community.

What this told me is that numbers do not provide the entire picture—especially when it comes to a large university. Even high school counselors and consultants don't know the real statistics. My experience taught me the importance of thoroughly researching admission information before ruling out a college or university. The best fit may be a university that seems too much of a stretch but in reality is one that is easily accessible.

Small vs. Large College

College size can have a major impact on success during the four years. Small colleges usually offer smaller classes and closer contact with professors. Large colleges and universities often have large lecture classes with little or no contact with a professor. It is often thought that an underachiever belongs in a small college. This is not necessarily true based on my experience. I think there are a number of issues to consider when choosing the right college for this type of child.

Finding a college with the right fit will be key to your child's success during their time in college. It is extremely important to visit colleges gauge what type of environment appeals to your child. My son Mike wanted to play football, which meant we looked at a lot of small liberal arts colleges mostly located in small towns. Most of the colleges were on 100 acres. When we visited one that was set on 200 acres, he said, "this feels like the right size to me." His final choice ended up being about 200 acres and located in a city. He has often stated that if he had ended up at one of the colleges in a small town, he would have transferred.

I had many reservations about sending Dave to a large university, but we included large universities on our college tour. On our first trip, we visited two colleges. The first one was a private college with a small engineering program. The labs hadn't been updated for decades. My son was disappointed with what he saw. Fortunately, the next day we went to a large public university and he became inspired by the beautiful campus with stately buildings, but more important, his enthusiasm soared when he toured the state-of-the-art labs in the engineering building. I realized that facilities were important to him. So, we focused our attention on the colleges that could afford state-of-the-art technology—this usually meant a public university.

How Colleges Evaluate Applicants

I know for certain not all colleges use the same standard for evaluating applicants. Currently, most seem to weigh more strongly the academic record over test scores. This usually disadvantages an underachiever unless they have become a student on the rise. At college information sessions, I have heard admission officers say they compare courses a student took to courses that were available. Again, this works against underachievers, who may not have had prerequisites to take honors and APs or who may have excelled later in high school. Then they compare a student's record against their peers from the same high school. So, if a college is popular at your child's high school, it may be more difficult for him to gain admission. Of course, colleges do review many other factors. They are basically trying to build a class. They do not want a class of clones. They need all types to fill different roles and from whom others can learn. Remember, most of the learning in college actually occurs outside the classroom. They need all different types of students. If your child has had a life experience that could set them apart, that may be the key to admission. Using that experience as a topic for the college essay would be one way to distinguish your child. Every college applicant compiles a list of reach, match, and safety schools. An underachiever may need more colleges on his list. If you include colleges that are a suitable match but not on his peers' wavelength, he may do surprisingly well in the admissions process.

Dave didn't take any APs in high school, although some were offered. Not only did he get accepted to a top university's engineering program, but he was also invited into one of its honors programs. Dave told me that most of the other students took numerous APs in high school. Dave's lack of AP classes did preclude the university from accepting him.

Resources for Choosing a College

I found tapping into college resources invaluable for determining which colleges would be a best fit for my boys. Keep an open mind. When compiling a list of Mike's colleges, the most important checkpoint was the D-3 college football list. Why put a lot of effort into a college that does not meet your child's needs? For us, that meant the college had to have a football team. Your child may also require a particular niche and that will be a key sorting tool in finding the right fit.

Naviance

Our high school had a system called Naviance, which was a college information computer program. It had links to college websites and also provided you with grades and scores of students from your child's school who were accepted to similar colleges. This was valuable information since colleges compare applicants against students from the same high school in terms of grades, scores, and strength of schedule. Since Naviance only lists colleges that students from your school have applied to, those colleges have passed a sort of cultural litmus test for students from a given high school. If a college is in your regional area but not on the list, proceed with caution—it may not meet the cultural requirements. I have found that the biggest problems with fit have been for students who have attended a college in an area that has a significant cultural difference. However, the good news—especially for underachievers—is that admittance may be a bit easier at one of those colleges since there will be little or no competition from high school peers. And if the college is far enough away, a student may also get extra points for geographic diversity.

Princeton Review

Princeton Review prints a college directory of approximately 360 colleges. This is a great resource since it gives you some information you might not find elsewhere, such as student surveys and how admissions views applications. This is a national directory, so at 360 colleges, it certainly misses many appropriate schools. Again, for the underachiever it may be advantageous to consider a college outside of that directory since it may not be as popular. However, it may be every bit as worthy and even more important, a suitable fit for your child.

US News Colleges

US News has an online college directory service that is inexpensive. I paid less than $20 for a year.

I especially like online services since you can switch back and forth from college websites to the information on the service. This program is especially helpful for conducting searches. You can search regionally, by major, etc. It also has a feature allowing you to compare colleges across various categories, such as scores, size, etc. I found this resource to be the most helpful of any I had used.

Colleges That Change Lives Book

Of course, what parent of an underachiever would be without this book as a resource. It features numerous fine colleges in various regions of the country. Unfortunately, these colleges may no longer be about changing lives. Mike applied to one of the colleges in the book. He also met with the football coach who supported him for admission. This was a D-3 college, so a coach does not have much influence. Mike was told that based on his high school record, they didn't think he could be successful. This college did not give much weight to his stellar performance at his postgraduate school. Nor did it seem to care much about his SAT scores. My impression was this college was no longer about changing lives. Now that admission numbers were up, they were about changing the image of the college. Hopefully, some of the colleges in this book still admit underachievers to give them an opportunity to change their lives. However, my son Mike went on to another college that did change his life. This college was not in the book, proving there are many other colleges that offer students an opportunity to start anew and help them succeed.

I highly recommend you tap into several resources. I found it helpful to compare information across the sources to determine validity or fill in a missing piece. If you use a college directory such as Princeton Review, your high school Naviance program, and US News College, you will be armed with all the information you need to find the right college situation for your child. When the fit works, the results can be awesome.

College—Setting Stage for Success

Grad School Tutors

I didn't realize how important it was to have access to grad students for tutoring until Mike went to college. As an engineering major, his course requirements included higher level math and physics. Mike needed help in physics and calculus. His college had a peer tutoring program, but they did not have tutors for these subjects. I was told that while a student may be able to sufficiently pass these subjects, they did not know them well enough to teach. Now, where would I find him help? I looked into tutoring companies but the nearest one was almost an hour away. That wouldn't be happening. Finally, I called the physics department and asked about tutors. The secretary gave me a couple of grad student names right away. The tutor I hired had a flexible schedule that worked well for Mike. He was also able to meet him on campus. Once Mike started working with the tutor, he was able to raise his grade and finished with a B. He continued working with the tutor the rest of the year. I believe the tutor helped develop Mike into the student he is today by giving him learning strategies that improved his study skills.

When Dave was looking at colleges, access to grad students became a prerequisite. Once he started, it became clear he needed a calculus tutor. His math teacher was not able to provide him with any leads. So, again, I contacted the math department and received some names of grad students. He raised his grade and continued working with the tutor. I believe a college with access to grad tutors is key for any student who may be taking higher level courses in math or science or other challenging classes. My boys may not have survived in their majors without grad tutor help.

eTutoring

eTutoring is a rather new concept. It is basically what it sounds like—tutoring by electronic means. Usually it involves email or skype. Having an eTutor can provide extra support for your child as he or she transitions into college. I think it works best if the child already has a relationship with the tutor. We coordinated an eTutor arrangement between Dave and his high school tutor for the start of his freshman year. There were a couple of goals we were trying to achieve—organization and tutoring help with papers. The organizational help involved working with Dave to establish a calendar that included his classes; due dates for tests, papers, and projects; and study times. The tutoring help involved working with the tutor on papers. This involved helping Dave understand the instructions and then form a thesis. The tutor was able to teach him to use the reference sources available through his university library. She also taught him how to cite sources correctly. eTutoring is actually more cost effective than regular tutoring since you do not have to pay for a entire hour if you do not need it. It is also much more flexible since there is not a physical appointment at a specific time. However, it does require the student to plan ahead. The tutor needs time to review and respond. My daughter used our tutor's service with great success. Since she was always pressed for time, it allowed her to ask for help at a time that worked best for her schedule. She was also able to get the attention she needed. Her papers greatly improved through this mentoring process.

Living Learning Communities

Living Learning communities are a residential opportunity that allows students of common interests to live together and participate in their themed interests. I first learned about Living Learning communities when touring a small liberal arts college. The tour guide pointed to a building called the Spanish House. He told us that students living there attempt to speak Spanish to each other and also share a weekly Spanish-speaking experience, such as a dinner out at a Mexican restaurant. I spoke with a woman whose son had studied engineering at our large state university. She said the turning point for him was when he moved into the tech dorm. Finally, he found like-minded students and fit in. It significantly enhanced his experience and helped him succeed. Dave was invited into a theme-based honors program at his large university. It is considered to be a state-of-the-art program and a model for our nation. We were worried about sending Dave to a large university, but he was passionate about this particular college. We were relieved when he was invited into this program, which is also a living learning community. All the students in the program live together. They each follow one of 12 themes. Through the theme-based program, they satisfy university requirements, enjoy field trips with peers, and participate in a capstone project. Dave adjusted seamlessly to college because of this program. It shrinks a large university into a small college. Basically, a living learning community presorts students to find similar types and places them together. Dave greatly benefitted. In a matter of a few days, he had met students sharing his interests. Under typical college circumstances, this could have taken months, maybe even a couple of years. I firmly believe a student who is happy socially will be more successful academically as long as they maintain the right balance. Dave also had friends who took similar classes, so he could access someone in his immediate vicinity if he needed help. The students in this program are typically highly motivated learners. In a Living Learning community, students benefit from the surrounding atmosphere. My son was never happier. I am certain this program provided the foundation for his success in college.

Team

Being part of a team is a useful advantage when starting college. Both my son Mike and daughter Brenda were on college teams. It created an immediate social group for them, which helped their transition to college. The older students on the teams offered advice and guidance. For instance, Mike attended a college that is surrounded by a dicey neighborhood. The older boys on the team told him that as long as he went out in a group, he would be okay. I was thankful for their guidance. If I had offered Mike the same advice, he would have accused me of being too safety conscious. But when he heard it from older teammates, he listened and took heed. Mike also looked to some of the upperclassmen as role models. He often told me about teammates who had made the Dean's List or who had a job lined up after college. Observing these students helped Mike prepare for future activities in college and even post-college. Academically, they were also able to offer guidance. The first semester of freshman year, Mike had a challenging final exam. One of the upperclassmen helped Mike review key points that were critical to pass. Being part of a team also taught Mike the importance of preparation and hard work. It taught him how to balance his academics with the demands of a sport. He learned what it means to be part of a team. Even though Mike played team sports throughout his life starting in kindergarten, all the lessons crystallized in college. The result was a formidable professional network post-college, which helped him while navigating his career. My daughter also has a laudable network. As a rower, she has contacts nationwide. In fact, many of her high school teammates ended up on teams at top colleges around the country.

Prospective employers recognize the skill set an athlete has developed will transfer directly to on-the-job performance. Athletes must commit time. They must prepare themselves. They must be able to take orders from their coaches. They must be able to play their position to the best of their ability to be part of the team. These are all the attributes an employer wants in a recruit. I highly recommend any student who can play a college sport to do so. They will get so much more out of it than they ever put into it. And it may just hold the key to future success.

Attendance Requirements

Some colleges have class attendance requirements. They may require attendance only during freshman year, but this can be extremely key to your child's success. I know it was for mine. Mike's college had freshman attendance requirements. And he learned pretty quickly these were serious rules. In a matter of a few weeks, one of his football teammates was sent home for lack of participation. This sent a strong message to him. We all know that class attendance contributes to educational success. Some professors base most testing on material contained in their lectures. Regardless, good students read the material first, then attend class where the material is reinforced by the professor. Then the student can go back and reread sections he or she did not understand well. The student also has the opportunity to question the professor or ask for points to be clarified that are not well understood. My son's college eased up on class attendance requirements after freshman year but by then habits were established. If you want your child to have the best chance of success, class attendance requirements may be key. Many students fail in their first year because they socialized too much and forgot their purpose for being there. Sometimes it is a matter of rebellion. Whatever the case, class attendance requirements certainly help support them during their first critical year in college.

Good Fit

You often hear that "good fit" is what you really want in a college. Many parents are concerned about the college name or the college's rating. Of course, these can be important but there are many great colleges. With my children, a suitable fit enabled them to excel. And this is especially important for underachievers. Mike's college was a perfect fit for him in every way—academically, socially, and environmentally. The academic fit worked because of the engineering school. This enabled him to enter his area of strengths immediately. The social fit occurred because the students were people he could relate to in many different ways. He was comfortable in the environment because he was in a relaxed, cooperative culture and had access to everything a city has to offer. And then there was football. The team worked out well for him regarding his relationships with both players and coaches, as well as the practice schedule. Fitting in and feeling comfortable provided Mike with the tools to be happy and excel.

Dave found a suitable college as well but for different reasons. His choice was to attend a large university that offered many opportunities. He was invited into a learning living program that created a small college environment. In a sense, Dave had the best of both worlds.

Outside Region

I think it is important to consider colleges outside your region, particularly if you are in a competitive area. We live in the Northeast in a small town about an hour from New York City. Our school system is one of the best in the state. We have bright students in the school system along with parents who continually encourage and support them. Children who can keep pace, benefit from this environment. I know my daughter did. However, my boys, coupled with learning disabilities and immaturity, suffered. Even though they are bright, they were told they weren't. I felt most colleges in our area would be equally intense, so they ended up south of the Mason Dixon line in the Washington, DC, area. People are every bit as bright down there, but the pace is a little slower, less intense and less competitive. Both of my boys excelled in this environment. Of course, they were also more mature and confident. And they had gained confidence. One word of caution: Be careful of cultures that are too different. Several students from our area went to the deep South and found it very difficult to fit in. You do not want to make that mistake with an underachiever. They are fragile. They might think the problem was they didn't like college; not that it wasn't the right fit. Finding the appropriate school the first time is so important for their success.

Setting: City vs. Country

By chance, Mike ended up at a college located in a city. In fact, it was the only one on his list that was not located in a rural or small-town environment. Very quickly, I realized what a strategic move it had been. First, he learned how to function in a city and navigate mass transit. He became comfortable in a city environment. Second, the city offered many diversions to college life. There was no reason to outgrow the college campus. Third, he had many opportunities for internships at his fingertips. Fourth, he was able to continue to live there after college where he had friends and was acclimated. Mike now says if he had gone to one of the other colleges, he probably would have transferred. He had multiple opportunities to experience and grow while attending college in a city. For a small-town boy, this is transformative. My younger son was also a short subway ride away from a major city. But since he was on a large university campus, he rarely ventured out. Even so, he learned to take the subway to the train station for trips home. In time, he took more advantage of what the city had to offer, sending them to city colleges relieved one of my big fears—getting them back after graduation to only live in my basement for years. You may laugh but it does happen, especially in our area. But they had a seamless move from college to work in the same city. While my older son's college placement was sheer luck, you may have guessed my younger sons was pure calculation. We always need to plan the next move with children who could just as easily lose momentum academically or otherwise.

Large vs. Small Engineering Schools

I have found a high number of high school underachievers become the future engineers of the world. That may be because while they are strong in math/science skills, they are weak in the verbal skills such as reading and writing that are important through high school. In case your child is an underachiever with an aptitude for or interest in engineering, I am including this mention about large vs. small engineering schools. Since my two sons were both engineering majors and one attended a large university while the other went to a small private college, I have some experience with both.

As I mentioned previously, Mike's college search was driven by football. Consequently, we looked at many small liberal arts colleges where he could major in physics and transfer to an engineering school under a 3/2 program. Fortunately, he ended up at one of the few D-3 football programs that also had an engineering school. I was quite impressed when I attended an engineering day open house. The classes were small, and the students received much one-on-one attention from the professors. There also seemed to be a lot of opportunity to work on projects with professors. I believe each student received a lot of hands-on experience.

Dave, however, was quite taken by the lab facilities that a large university offered. Especially where technology is concerned, the large state universities are hard to beat. They have the money to ensure their labs have the most up-to-date equipment. This was not true of some of the smaller programs. However, in a large program, classes are larger and there may not be as much one-on-one time with a professor or even hands-on learning. -Be sure to consider this when researching schools.

The jury is still out on which engineering program served our sons' best—the smaller or larger one. But I think it ended in a tie because each one had the right fit for their individual needs. The end result was they both earned engineering degrees and are now building careers in the field.

3/2 Engineering

Mike always had weak verbal skills (reading and writing) but was strong in math and science. Consequently, we felt engineering might be the path for him just as it was for his father and grandfather. Since he wanted to play college football, that left out most engineering schools. So, we were ecstatic when I first learned of 3/2 Engineering through exploring various liberal arts college websites. Basically, 3/2 engineering is a program offered by a number of liberal arts colleges, which enables a student to pursue a liberal arts education for three years and then transfer to an engineering school for the last two years. The student earns a dual degree—one from the liberal arts college and another from the engineering school. Typically, a student majors in physics and there is a GPA minimum to be eligible for the program. Liberal arts colleges have partnered with a number of engineering schools. The partnerships vary but often include such prestigious universities as Columbia University, Washington University in St. Louis, and Case Western.

We thought 3/2 Engineering might be a great option for our son Mike whose strengths have always been in math and science. However, he ended up at a college that had a variety of schools, including engineering through which he could earn a degree in four years.

I know of one student who has used the 3/2 Engineering option and it is working out quite well for a couple of reasons. First, he is at Columbia University, which is located in New York City. Having the city as his playground made the transfer process much more attractive. Second, his liberal arts college is a short drive away, so he still sees his friends on weekends. Columbia also houses the transfer students together, which helps make their transition much easier.

Reflecting on the 3/2 Engineering program for Mike, we know it would not have worked out as planned. As a football player, he would have wanted to play his last semester of eligibility and he would not have wanted to leave his friends during senior year. Although he could have done 4/2 Engineering, which would have involved a lot of extra tuition costs. But more important, Mike was successful in college because functioned in an area of his strengths. If he had gone to a Liberal arts college, he would have been required to take classes in the area of his weaknesses. More than likely, he would not have had the GPA to transfer to a top engineering school.

Explore College Websites

There is much to learn about a college by exploring its website. You may discover a good match for your child or you may realize a college that you should remove from the list. I certainly recommend exploring the college website of every college you are seriously considering for your child. The first thing I like to do is read the mission statement. Then, I read the welcome letter from the college president and read his or her biography. Knowledge from those sources can help set the tone. Further, review the academics and extracurricular activities offered. If there's a link to the student newspaper, peruse it or pick one up on the college visit. That's a good way to find out more of what is happening on campus and what the students are like. If your child is interested in a particular major, explore it in detail. By exploring the engineering pages at my son's college, I learned the engineering school admits almost twice as many students as the percentage advertised for the entire university. That information could have made the difference between applying and not applying because with that new information, Dave's admittance was almost certain. There are also numerous other items you will learn about a specific college to enable you to tailor your application if using the college's own application rather than the Common App. For instance, you may discover there is a certain club sport on campus that your son would fit into. Dave had been taking boxing lessons so when we noticed that there was a boxing club, we made sure to discuss his interest in the sport on one of the short essays required. I also encourage you to read things you think may not apply to your child. For instance, Dave was not interested in being considered for an honors program and we didn't think he would qualify if he had been interested. Consequently, I missed seeing the information on the theme-based scholars program Dave was invited into. It turns out students can also apply to be considered for it. But we had skipped over that program because we didn't think it would be a possibility for him. That's another lesson; don't underestimate your child in the college process. Dave had been in such a competitive high school program that we just didn't realize how strongly he matched up against others outside his school community. In a state university setting, he was competitive.

Pre-college Programs—Turtle Camp

Pre-college programs offer an excellent way to begin the adjustment to college. Many colleges offer them. Many are modeled on an outward bound type experience but at levels appropriate for the various participants. My son, Dave, was invited to participate in a leadership camp at his university. After a brief initiation, the group headed to a nearby state park where they spent four days camping and participating in a variety of high adventure experiences. The idea behind these programs is the students will arrive on campus already knowing a group of other students. This may only serve as a short-term social adjustment after which students find other friends with whom they have more in common; or continue to pursue the relationships for a longer period of time. During the program, counselors took the opportunity to explain college life and answer questions. This helped allay many of my son's fears. In addition, since Dave is an Eagle Scout with camping skills, he was able to assume leadership in the group. He realized he knew some things the other students didn't know, and it raised his self-esteem. This turned out to be key because once he moved into his living learning community, he was a bit intimidated by the fact that most of the students had taken numerous AP courses. He felt behind academically. However, because his self-esteem had been raised, he realized it didn't mean the other students were also smarter than him. The pre-college program provided Dave with the boost he needed to start college feeling comfortable.

It's Time to Go to Work

Role of Internships

Internships have become an almost mandatory requirement before entering the workplace. The benefit is twofold. It provides students an opportunity to test themselves to learn if a particular field or company is appropriate. Likewise, it offers a company an opportunity to preview the type of employee a student might be and where in the organization he or she might best fit.

Colleges host career fairs on a regular basis. It is a helpful place to start seeking internships. In fact, it is where Mike found his. He was hired by an engineering company the summer before his final semester. By that time, he was ready for a work experience. They were paying him, too, thus it gave him an added incentive. He was placed in the estimating area. Estimators arranged bids on a project. He learned a lot while working for the company; unfortunately, he wasn't hired, as the company was not hiring when he graduated. However, his estimating experience was critical in securing the position at where he currently works. The large construction company needed someone in estimating and he was highly qualified. Mike believes the internship was key to his employment and, based on his experience, it is mandatory.

Don't discount applying online for an internship, as Dave did at the National Institutes of Health. A few months after submitting his application, he received a form letter stating he was one of the "best candidates," so he advanced to the next step. But don't call us, we'll call you. After a few weeks had passed, he received a call for a phone interview. The next day, he received an email with an internship offer in engineering.

Getting the Job

When Mike was ready to enter the job market the following January, his internship company could not afford to hire him. We were concerned that by ending his internship in December, Mike would be off the regular hiring cycle. But we discovered opportunities still existed.

Mike began his job search in earnest in mid-January after his internship ended. He was in the process of interviewing with several construction companies when an opportunity arose at a large construction company where one of his friends was in a Builders in Training program. The friend arranged a meeting for Mike with a vice president. Luckily, there was a need for someone in the estimating area and since he already had experience, he was a match.

Mike liked everything he heard about this company and its projects. They made him the first offer and placed him into a Builders in Training program. This required a rotation over two years between estimating, project engineer, and project supervisor. Mike started in the estimating area two months after he began his search. His predecessor spent only a few months there, which is the norm, but Mike was doing so well they kept him for over a year. During that time, he received two raises, plus a bonus. During his review, he received a perfect score and a promise to fast track him in his career. His supervisor told him he was the best recruit they had had up to that point. This encouragement had provided even more motivation for Mike to succeed. He now understands the connection between hard work and success and is committed to his job and the company.

Dave, too, is employed in an engineering career that has a future and fuels his passion. After two summers at the National Institutes of Health, Dave realized it was not the place for him. However, his experience and Eagle Scout rank helped him secure the position with a military government entity. Currently, he is involved in designing military vehicles, which are state-of-the-art and involve ingenuity. His career is intellectually challenging and contributes to the safety of the world. The seeds of success were always present. While some teachers may have missed them, we, as his parents, recognized his potential and did not veer from our objective: helping our son succeed.

Conclusion

"They find their way." I can't tell you how many times I have heard the phrase from professionals, whether they be teachers, counselors, or somebody else. And I do not agree that kids will find their way on their own. Of course, there are many so called ways in the world—many of which we would not want for our children. Students who are working below their potential may be more prone to finding the less desirable ways because of their frustration over their failures. Let's not forget, by definition, underachievers are working well below their capability. They are usually smart, but something is holding them back. Therefore, parents need to help them remove all obstacles preventing our children from excelling. We cannot abandon them no matter their age. However, we have less ability to influence our children as they grow. This is why we need to be involved when they are young and continue to stay involved.

Quite honestly, I wasn't sure what the end result would be with either boy, but I put my faith in the process. We tried to solve their problems at every juncture through various support systems and interventions.

Several strategies were more effective than others, including:

Tutors and academic support

College with access to grad students for tutors

Postgraduate year

Sports team

Living learning community in college

City environment for college

It was important that we devised strategies and tactics at the start, knowing our objective at the end of the process. We always tried to keep the boys steered in that direction. We also tried to stay at least one step ahead of them so we could be prepared to deal with any obstacles. I also think it helped that we never alienated either boy. They always knew we supported them 100% and only wanted the best for them. They did not feel the need to rebel or punish us. In their hearts, they always knew we love them.

I hope you have learned something that will help your child become better prepared for college and beyond. Please keep this book as a reference because you may find it helpful at different stages. But most of all, when you no longer need it, please pass it on to someone who does. Remember, your child is not the only student who is underperforming. As one educator told me, "It's a growth industry."

Keep in mind, underachievers can and do become successful adults. By using strategies in this book, your child will be guided toward his strengths, resulting in success, satisfaction, and happiness.

Most important, never give up. Your child, no matter how old, will always benefit from your guidance and most of all, your love. **Parenting never ends.**

Author Bio

B.A. King is an author of several books, including *The College Plan for Underachievers*. After a career in public affairs, she traded the workplace for the home front to raise three children, two diagnosed with ADHD. She has faced many of the same struggles parents reading this book deal with every day. Her mission is to help them navigate through their child's challenging wonder years to a successful outcome. She lives in a New York City suburb with her husband that has been their home for over 25 years.

Contact: author@barbaraanneking.com

www.ingramcontent.com/pod-product-compliance
Lightning Source LLC
Chambersburg PA
CBHW021127080526
44587CB00012B/1167